BLOGGING WHILE DISABLED

HOW TO MAKE MONEY WRITING FROM A WHEELCHAIR

SYLVIA LONGMIRE

PRINTED IN THE UNITED STATES OF AMERICA

Visit my world at www.spintheglobe.net

First edition published in 2020.

Book design by Sylvia Longmire.

Editing by Victoria J. Yore.

Cover Image: ©Sylvia Longmire

ISBN: 978-1-7345113-1-4

CONTENTS

AUTHOR'S NOTE

Have you ever purchased an electronic device and balked when you saw an instruction manual the size of a phone book? Then thanked your lucky stars when you saw the little tri-fold "quick start" guide? I'm happy to inform you that this guide is what you're about to read.

Starting a blog or any sort of writing endeavor is actually quite easy. However, becoming a real expert at either takes time, effort, and emotional (and sometimes significant financial) investment. I could drown you in the details of WordPress plug-ins, search engine optimization, social media strategies, and Google Analytics exploitation to this end. I have deliberately chosen not to for several reasons explained below.

In *Blogging While Disabled*, I will share tons of tips on how to become a better writer, how to create a blog and start a small business, and how to promote your work. I'm proficient in many of the skills required to be a successful blogger, but I am by no means an expert on every single aspect. Fortunately, I have many friends and colleagues who are. At the end of this book, you will find an appendix with links to additional resources for all the significant aspects of writing and blogging. This will make it easier for you to refer back to them when you need them.

Absolutely anyone can use this book to kick-start a new career in writing or blogging. However, in several instances, I make a note of things relevant to people with disabilities and wheelchair users for two main reasons. First, we have the highest rate of unemployment and underemployment of any American demographic group. This is partly due to employment discrimination, but mainly because physical limitations often prevent us from taking advantage of more traditional employment opportunities.

Second, working from home as a writer is how I've been making a living for over a decade, so I know it can be done. This book is primarily meant to encourage wheelchair users to express their knowledge and passions through writing, and help them potentially earn income in ways they might not have thought otherwise possible.

This world is continuously changing and updating, so it's a constant learning process. I highly encourage you to make the most of Google, and conduct additional research on your own for the best options to improve your blog and writing opportunities. These resources will get you off on the right foot, if only figuratively speaking, and just be aware that the things you will learn in this book are just the start of an exciting new adventure.

1 WHY START A BLOG?

There are several excellent reasons to start a blog, and just as many good reasons not to. I'll begin this introductory chapter with the journey to starting my first blog, which helped me understand what all of those reasons are. Now I can share them with you.

I'm currently a professional (i.e., paid) writer. However, I wasn't always a good writer, and have zero professional training. I took one technical writing class in college as part of my marketing degree, and one basic English class as a freshman. I've always been a proficient and avid reader, so my vocabulary and grammar skills have typically been excellent. However, outside of high school literature classes and college papers, no one had ever given me instruction or provided guidance on how to write a story for the general public.

During my final assignment in the Air Force, I worked as a counterterrorism analyst. Unlike analysts in other government jobs, I did not attend formal training to become an analyst. When I signed in at my new base and started my new job, I had no idea what I was supposed to do. It was then that I knew I had to learn from the fantastic professionals around me. I read everything they were writing and took note of their style. I tried to imitate that as best I could. At first, I failed pretty often. However, with strong feedback and guidance, I got better every time.

After I was medically retired from the Air Force in 2005 and concluded four years of civilian work as a threat analyst in 2009, I wanted to keep writing. However, the analytical style I had been using was useless for the general public. I had no mentor and no idea how to become a freelance writer, let alone how to pitch magazines or newspapers. So, I did what I thought made sense — I bought the *Associated Press Style Guide* and started teaching myself how to write for regular people.

Over the next couple of years, I sought out the writing of the best journalists covering my areas of expertise: the drug war in Mexico and border security. They didn't all write the same way, but there were enough similarities in their writing that I could try to do the same thing I did in the Air Force. I imitated them as best I could while slowly injecting my personal style. A few years later, in 2011, I would have my first traditionally published full-length book under my belt, and my second book was published three years later. Both *Cartel* and *Border Insecurity* are still selling on Amazon.com today.

In 2015, my life turned upside down. I got divorced, my children started living with their father, and for the first time in ten years, I was living by myself. I traveled extensively before I got married, quite frequently by myself, but hardly traveled at all during my marriage. Now that I had a considerable amount of free time, I needed to do something to heal from my divorce. I decided to give traveling a try once more. However, there was a small kink in my plan—I was now a full-time wheelchair user.

Slowly, I learned what I needed to do to travel with my electric scooter (at the time), and I began planning international trips. The first few went very well, so I planned some more. The more I traveled, the more my confidence increased. After the first year of my solo wheelchair travels, I reminded myself, *Hey, you're a writer. Why aren't you writing about all of this?* In the course of conducting my destination research, I had come across the blogs of several other wheelchair travelers. I thought, *If they can do this, why can't I?* And so, Spin the Globe was born.

Just like my other writing endeavors, my accessible travel blog was not a winner right out of the gate. I had no real goal for my blog; it was more of a journal than anything else. For my first few trips, I would write a post about what I did that day. I'd describe the things I had seen and done, which were basically nothing anyone cared about other than close friends and family members. I look back now at my initial blog posts and groan. However, I also feel some pride at how much I've grown and improved through experience.

I wish I could tell you the specific moment I realized that blogging had the potential to produce income. It wasn't a lightbulb moment, but rather a learning process. I started reading more and more travel blogs written not just by wheelchair users, but by a variety of people. It became easier to tell who was blogging for the fun of it and who was blogging as a serious business endeavor.

During my second year as a travel blogger, I attended my very first blogging conference, specifically the Travel Bloggers Exchange (TBEX). This is one of the largest travel blogging conferences in the world, and to say attending was like drinking from a fire hose is an understatement. I heard terms like "SEO" and "plug-in" for the first time. I didn't know what Mediavine was, or why people were killing themselves trying to join it. I had no idea what the difference was between page views, unique users, and sessions, or why brands cared how much of them you had every month.

Over time, and by attending other conferences like that one, I was able to figure all of this stuff out, and much more. But more importantly, I was able to set goals, understand precisely why I was blogging, and realize who I wanted to reach with my blog. I also learned exactly what I needed to do to start making money with my blog.

There are two primary reasons to start a blog. The first one is entirely for personal reasons. This could be for the enjoyment of writing, being able to express yourself, to tell stories, or to keep an online journal to share with friends and family. People who blog for personal reasons tend not to care who reads their blog. They also frequently use blogs as a repository for photographs, family stories, and vacation notes.

The second primary reason to start a blog is to generate income by serving a specific audience. This is the harder road. Professional bloggers almost always write about things they enjoy, so there's definitely an element of fun. However, they also aim to write about things for an existing (and hopefully growing) audience. They write to provide information that will be useful and sought after. Finally, they write in a way that makes this information easy to find online.

Whether your goal for starting a blog is for personal enjoyment or to make money, this guide will help you. What makes this book different is a wheelchair user and a person with a disability wrote it primarily for other wheelchair users and people with disabilities. The basic process for anyone starting a blog is the same. However, the *why* is sometimes different, and the *how* sometimes presents some unique challenges.

You may need to become familiar with dictation software if typing is a challenge (like it is for me). You may need physical assistance in creating and embedding media, like photos and videos. If you've never written something for public consumption, you may need to become familiar with tools like spell check and grammar check at best, or in the worst-case scenario, a quick online course in basic writing skills. Always keep in mind that if you want to be a professional blogger someday, you get out of it what you put into it. However, as I've demonstrated, *you don't need to be a trained writer to succeed at blogging.*

Statistically, people with disabilities have the highest unemployment rate in America. Although many people with disabilities have the potential to work from home or start their own businesses, we are continuously discouraged by both society and the professional world from doing so, receiving the message that we're not capable because we lack the physical or mental capacity. While there are tons of books and articles with suggestions for how non-disabled people can do these things, few resources are offering the same opportunities for people with disabilities. My goal is to provide that for you with this book.

I need to be very clear and explain that blogging will very rarely make you wealthy. It takes time and a lot of hard work to start making money from blogging. Not only do you need to hone your writing skills, but you have to become familiar with the business, the competition, and the logistics of growing your audience. You have to develop a personal brand, and learn how to familiarize people with it. When people think about your blog's topic, you want them to think about YOU first.

All this being said, the voice of wheelchair users and people with disabilities is vastly underrepresented in the blogging world, like pretty much everywhere else. But chances are that you have a story to tell, and that many other people with experiences similar to yours need to hear them. Odds are also good that you have extensive knowledge of or experience with something—the Civil War, race cars, flowers, makeup, you name it—that other people are also interested in. Remember that every single blogger starts with one post.

I've already proven that you don't have to start as a natural writer, or even a good writer. That can be learned, and so can the logistics of posting and marketing. Truly successful blogging is all about providing answers that enough people are searching for. With that, I'll give you some guidance on how to determine what other people are interested in, and whether or not you can provide some of those answers.

2 PICKING THE PERFECT BLOG TOPIC

You've thought about the different reasons for starting a blog, and you believe you have the motivation and (potential) skills to take the next step. Now it's time to make a huge decision—what you want to write about. If you're only going to blog for fun, then you can write about absolutely anything you want. However, if you eventually want to monetize your blog, there are certain things you should take into consideration when choosing a blog topic.

Based on my experience as a blogger and an active participant in the general blogging community, there are four rules I think new bloggers should follow when selecting a topic.

1. Write about what you know. One can acquire expertise in many different ways. Sometimes it's through reading and study, and sometimes it's through personal experience. The world's top experts on the American Revolution certainly didn't live through it. However, you'd better believe that they've read close to everything that's ever been written about it. Bloggers who write about golf have likely been playing for many years, have used a wide variety of equipment, and have played at dozens of different golf courses, probably around the world.

Does this mean that you have to be an expert at something? Not necessarily. But if you want readers to perceive you as an authentic blogger, you should select a topic for your blog you know quite a lot about. Just because you're a wheelchair user or have a disability doesn't automatically mean that's what you should write about. However, who knows more about what your life experience is like than you? You can write about spinal cord injury, or cerebral palsy, or multiple sclerosis if you live with any of these conditions.

Again, just because you have a disability doesn't mean that you don't have other areas of expertise. You can write about hobbies that you've practiced for years, publish book or movie reviews, or talk about NASCAR races that you've watched. Seriously, the possibilities are endless. The important thing is to pick something to write about on which you have at least some level of authority through education or experience.

2. Find a comfortable niche. Not too long ago, I was taking a look at comments on a post in a Facebook group about blogging. Someone was asking for advice from bloggers who were making at least $2,000 a month through their blogs. I'm not making nearly that much (yet), so I was really curious what other bloggers had to say. Then I saw a comment from a woman who is making $400,000 a year just from her blog.

My jaw dropped. I wondered immediately, what is she blogging about? Food? Parenting? Fashion? If she's blogging about travel, I wanted to know what I could do better. After all, these are the most popular categories where you can find most of the top blogging moneymakers. It turned out she's not blogging about any of those things—not even close. She writes about poultry. Specifically, she writes about things like how to raise chickens and ducks and geese in your backyard, and what to do with their eggs. She writes books about it and has a TV show about it, and she even sells poultry supplements through her blog.

What is the secret to her success? She found a great blogging niche. There are currently over 600 million blogs worldwide, and 2 billion blog posts are published every year. Looking at those numbers, it seems impossible that anyone can compete in this industry. Yet, here you have this blogger making almost half a million dollars every year blogging about chickens and ducks and geese. The trick is to find a specialty, or a corner known as a niche, for your blog topic.

For example, there are tons and tons and of travel blogs out there. However, there aren't nearly as many blogs about accessible travel. This is why I'm able to compete and succeed. There are also tons of food blogs and parenting blogs and fashion blogs. However, you'll tend to find success stories from bloggers to focus on one particular type of food, like Cajun food or sushi or vegan or gluten-free diets. Parenting niche blogs will talk about co-sleeping or twins or adopted children. Fashion niche blogs will focus on luxury brands or plus sizes or children's clothing.

The art of picking the right blog topic is to make sure there is an existing audience that is not too big, but also not too small. For example, there's nothing wrong with wanting to write about life in a wheelchair in general. However, you may have more success writing about life in a wheelchair with a spinal cord injury, or life in a manual wheelchair, or life in a power wheelchair, or life traveling in a wheelchair, or life as a parent in a wheelchair.

While it may sound counterintuitive, don't be afraid to create a blog on a very specific subject. Google wants to know that you are an expert on one particular thing. The more you write about that particular topic, the more well-known you will become as the go to expert. Also, your blog and posts will come up more frequently in Google searches when people look for information relevant to your topic. It's much easier to start out narrow, then grow by broadening your subject matter rather than the other way around.

3. Choose a topic with room to grow. The last thing you want to do when selecting a blog topic is to limit yourself right off the bat. There are certain things you can only write so much about, and you want a topic where you have room to create a lot of content in the months and years to come.

For example, you may have watched the movie *Gremlins* five hundred times and can recite every word of dialogue by heart. You know the names of every person in the cast and crew and every possible statistic there is to know about the film. Because you're clearly an expert on

Gremlins, you decide you want to start a blog about it because, hey, that's your passion.

But how many blog posts can you write over a considerable period into the future about an old movie that has no planned sequels and limited merchandise on the shelves? How many people in the world are actively searching for information about *Gremlins*? How many brands would want to partner with you to advertise or sell their *Gremlins*-related merchandise on your blog? This isn't to say you shouldn't create a blog about *Gremlins*. But if your goal is to make money from writing, you may want to consider another blog topic.

Think about subjects that have the potential to continue or change or expand in the future. You should also be able to approach potential topics from several different angles. For example, I plan to travel in the future, so I know I'll be able to write about new destinations for my blog. However, during times when I'm at home, I can write about accessible cruises, provide travel tips for wheelchair users, or create other posts that aren't directly tied to something I'm doing in the short-term.

Ask yourself, *Can I write 500 blog posts about this topic? 1,000 posts?* If the answer is no, then you may want to consider another topic. I have published over 250 blog posts in the last four years, and I have plenty of room to grow and expand. This is because I'm constantly traveling, but also because the travel industry and the space in it for wheelchair users is always changing. Always remember that Google is about *authority*. The more you write about a topic, the more you will be perceived as an authority during Google searches.

4. Be capable of providing value to readers. People who read and follow blogs find value in different things they offer. Some blog readers simply like a good story and enjoy being entertained. Food lovers, parents, and vegetarians are always in search of tasty recipes that suit their meal needs, and certainly have their favorite go-to food blogs. Everyone travels differently, so seniors, Gen Z, minority groups, and wheelchair users will look for blogs that provide information relevant to their travel needs.

When you're examining your options for blog topics, think about what value your articles can provide to potential readers. That value can be overt. For example, if you are writing a review on front caster wheels for manual wheelchairs, you're providing concrete recommendations for people who have a particular need. However, the value of a blog post can also be more subtle. A caregiver for a person with ALS can derive a lot of value from an article written by another caregiver in a similar situation. Testimonial blogs can go a long way towards helping people in certain communities feel understood and visible.

Later in this book, I will talk about how potential readers can find your blog and your articles. Part of how you get discovered in the Internet jungle is to answer questions that many people are asking. Think about subjects with which you're familiar. When you first took an interest in these things, what questions did you have? What are some common things that people ask you about your hobbies or disability, or issues you could potentially write a blog about? There are many ways to find out what questions people are commonly asking. If your blog posts can answer these questions, then you have the potential to succeed as a blogger.

Keep in mind that you don't have to be the most engaging or humorous or entertaining person on the Internet. Sometimes, blog readers follow the writer because of a personal connection, especially if posts are more narrative in form. However, more often than not, people follow a blog because of the information it contains. It's important for authenticity that you speak from your personal experience, but if you write with the goal of making money in the long term, write less about you and more for your audience.

3 CREATING YOUR BLOG

You've made some hard decisions, and you know exactly what you want to blog about. You also know who you want to write for, and maybe have a general idea of what you want to say. In this chapter, I'll help you get started on turning your idea into a website where you can share your thoughts and ideas.

Picking a blog name

One of the most important decisions you'll make when starting a blog is choosing a name, and subsequently the URL (website address). This isn't something you want to rush. While technically you can change your blog name whenever you want, changing your website address, social media pages, business cards, and anything else that bears your blog's name takes a lot of time and effort. It's best to get it right the first time.

When considering a blog name, there are a few basic elements you want to try to incorporate. First, your blog name should somehow reflect its main topic. This doesn't mean you explicitly have to use a word describing the blog category in your blog name (e.g., travel, food, parenting, wheelchair, disability, etc.). I love a fun play on words for blog titles. For example, I chose my blog title of Spin the Globe because it implies both travel and the movement of my power wheelchair.

Another thing to consider is the length of your blog title. Shorter is better for a few reasons. First, it's easier to remember. Second, it takes up less space on business cards and promotional materials. Third, it's easier to design a clean main blog page with less text. All that being said, a longer title might make it easier to find a good available URL.

The term URL stands for universal resource locator, but it's simply your website address. I'll explain later how to purchase and register a website address for your blog, which is called a domain name. For now, you need to find a domain name that's available for purchase, which may affect your choice for a blog name. It's also a good idea to write down what your blog's name would look like as a website address, with all the letters together and no spaces. For example, a blog titled "Linda as Sam's Mom" would appear as www.lindaassamsmom.com, which could be problematic for both the appearance of the word *ass*, and the aesthetic jumble of similar letters.

It's something of an art form to pick a blog name that's unique enough to easily find an available identical domain name, yet straightforward enough to understand its primary subject matter. If your first choice for a domain name isn't available, you have a couple of options. The companies that will sell you a domain and host your blog site offer several choices for what's called a top-level domain (TLD), or those three letters after the dot at the end of your domain name.

The ideal for many businesses is to end their website address with .com (dot com). However, finding the .com domain you want can be challenging. When I looked for the domain availability for Spin the Globe, the .com version was already taken. I decided against my second choice, which was to change my blog name. Instead, I opted for the .net TLD. The third most common TLD is .org, and while this is primarily used by non-profit groups and other community-type organizations, technically anyone can use it.

There are pros and cons to using a TLD other than .com. The main benefit is that it will be easier to find an available domain that you want. The biggest downside is that your blog readers may assume your blog ends in .com. If they remember your blog name without seeing it written down, they may type it into the browser address bar with the .com TLD and wonder why they can't find your blog. If you create an email account through your host that's associated with your domain, your email address will also end in .net or .org, and emails will bounce back to the sender if they use .com instead. If you have the slightest amount of emotional flexibility when it comes to choosing a blog URL with a .com TLD, I would highly recommend going that route.

My suggestion is that you try to find as many blogs as possible about your preferred topic and see what names they're using. Think about what you like or don't like about their blog names (Clever? Funny? Too long? Misleading?), and figure out how you can make yours stand out. Next, search for your preferred domain name to see what's available. I like Google's domain search tool because it offers multiple variations on your preferred blog name if it's not available.

Choosing a site host

A host is a company that provides a virtual place for you to park your domain name and your blog's website. While you will use software and a platform (which I'll discuss below) to create what your blog will look like, all of that information needs to be stored somewhere. A site host will charge you an annual fee for the rights to your domain name (usually around $10/year), and either a monthly or annual fee to host the blog itself.

There are several factors you need to consider when choosing a site host. There are several hosts to choose from, and they offer different packages based on your anticipated needs for your blog. Will your blog be very simple, with mostly text and just a few photos? Will you be posting a lot of photos and videos that require more memory and processing speed? Will you be selling things through your blog that require eCommerce support? Even if you don't need certain capabilities now, it's good to find a host that will allow your blog to grow without having to switch hosts.

The blog Learn to Code with Me offers a great guide on what to look for in a good site host. Things to consider include security, reliability, good customer service, and reasonable prices. WhoIsHostingThis? offers a great step-by-step guide for comparing hosts, and helping you choose which host would work for you based on your needs and budget.

After you've selected a web host, you can purchase your domain through them, then purchase your hosting plan.

Choosing a platform

You have a blog name, a domain name and website address for your blog, and a host where you can store your blog's information. Now, it's time to create your blog! Before you can start picking curtains, furniture, and paint colors, you have to pick a house—otherwise known as a blogging platform.

A platform is the software and associated tools that you'll use to create your blog. When you choose how your blog will look, write new posts, and upload photos, you'll use this platform. You can also use the platform to monitor your blog's data, like your monthly traffic and security-related information. Some platforms are separate from, but work in conjunction with, web hosts. Other platforms are integrated with a host, like an all-in-one package.

Three popular platforms combine blog design with hosting: SquareSpace, Wix, and Weebly. They tend to be easier to use for beginners. However, they offer fewer options for customization. WordPress is by far the most popular platform for bloggers, and is used by 35 percent of websites in existence today. Downloading and using WordPress is free, but you have to arrange and pay for hosting separately. It's a bit more complicated to use than the other options, but WordPress also offers an almost infinite number of tutorials and community support.

I use WordPress for all of my blogs. However, WordPress may not be right for you. Make a Website has a great comparison tool to help you understand what each platform does, how it works, and which one will meet your needs. However, I would very strongly recommend using WordPress from the start, even if you have to pay someone to help you set it up. If monetizing a blog is your goal, WordPress offers the most flexibility and ease of use in the long term.

Also, make sure you understand the difference between the WordPress.com and WordPress.org sites. If you want independent control of your blog and have a site hosting plan set up, then the .ORG site is the way to go. I recommend the .ORG site in 99 percent of cases for new bloggers. The .COM site offers hosting services, some of which are free. This may be beneficial for small hobby bloggers. However, available services and features for blogs on this platform will be extremely limited. You may not even need to use the .ORG site at all (I don't), as many site hosts offer their own independent installation of WordPress.

Choosing the right design template

The great thing about today's blog creation platforms is that you don't have to start from scratch, meaning you don't have to stare at a blank page and figure out what to put there. You literally have hundreds of design templates to choose from, which can initially seem overwhelming. Where do you even start?

Fortunately, there are several tools that can help you narrow down your template choices. First, make use of your platform's categories. For example, they try to group templates that work better for photographers (more photos), food writers (recipe posts), and sellers (online shops). This doesn't mean you should limit yourself to travel templates as a travel blogger; it's just to help you get started.

Another thing to think about is how the template theme fits your blog's subject matter. Do you want something whimsical and light, or more edgy with darker tones? If you're writing about bees, maybe consider a theme with yellow as a primary color, or greens and blues if you're writing about the outdoors. If your blog will be more of a journal, keep the theme simple, with few elements to distract from your words.

Finally, consider what you want the experience to be like for your blog readers. If pictures are an essential element of your blog topic, remember that too many will slow down your blog's page load times. Your blog page will look stunning, but readers may not stick around if it takes too long for those photos to appear on their phones or computer screens. Think about who your readers are. Most themes today are set up to be mobile-friendly and accessible (which is a legal requirement). But are you writing for people with visual impairments, or some physical limitation that makes clicking on text or small hot spots difficult? Keep this in mind.

Your primary goal for a blog that you ultimately want to monetize is to offer your readers *value.* Ask yourself if your design theme allows you to do that, whether that value takes the form of stories, advice, video tutorials, or products. Also, always remember that WordPress themes are free to use. You only have to pay to upgrade the theme to a deluxe version, which will just have more bells and whistles. Many top-notch bloggers are extremely successful using free themes.

Navigating a sea of plug-ins

After you've created your blog's foundation using a theme template provided by your platform, the next step is to make it your own, both by customizing it and making it work for you. The tools that will help you with this are called plug-ins (like plugging something into a jack or socket, and magically something starts happening). There are plug-ins for virtually everything you could possibly do with your blog, ranging from how it looks to how it operates.

For example, there are plug-ins that make inserting photos easier, give you more font options for your posts, and help compress your images to help them load faster. There are plug-ins that can help you improve the accessibility of your blog. Some of them you have to purchase or subscribe to, but many of them are free. It's easy to do a Google search for the most popular or useful plug-ins. Just make sure you read the fine print in the description for each plug-in to make sure it's compatible with your platform before you download and install it.

4 WRITING FOR YOUR BLOG

But Sylvia...I'm a terrible writer. How can I create a blog if I can't write? Easy—you learn. Many of us are not natural writers. We know how to communicate and have a conversation, but when it comes to putting pen to paper (literally or figuratively), a lot of us can't remember the most fundamental things we learned in our high school English classes.

You don't have to be a professional writer to start a blog. You don't even have to be a great writer. While that certainly helps, the most important thing you need to do as a blogger is to *provide value for your audience*. Trust me, I've seen many blogs where the writing is atrocious, but the blogger still commands hundreds of thousands of monthly page views. How is this possible? Easy—the value of the content they provide overrides any shortcomings their audience might perceive in their writing.

That being said, it may take a while for people to find the value in your brand-new blog. If no one knows who you are, the easiest way to turn off a new reader is with lousy writing. People will find it hard to focus on your content if they have to struggle through numerous (and continuous) spelling and grammatical errors. Your text will also be harder to follow if your use of punctuation is lacking. Few people will take you seriously as an authority on a topic if your blog posts read like

1,000-word text messages. This chapter will focus on getting you ready to write credibly for your blog.

Basic writing tips

You don't have to be Ernest Hemingway to start a blog. However, depending on what the ultimate goal is for your blog, you may need to brush up on some basic writing skills. First, ask yourself how you want your readers to perceive you. If your blog is just for a hobby, only for sharing with friends and family, and you simply intend to have fun with it, you may be content with writing in text-speak. However, if you want total strangers to read it, appreciate it, and take you seriously, then you may want to investigate some ways to improve your writing.

One of the easiest ways to assess your current writing skills is to have a friend or family member read some samples. Write out three potential blog posts that are least 500 words long. Put some effort into it, including the use of spell check, grammar check, Grammarly, or whatever tools are available with your word processing software. Then comes the hardest part—asking for an honest critique and not taking it personally.

You want your reviewer to tell you a few things. First, was the spelling, punctuation, and grammar used properly? Did your ideas flow smoothly? Was it easy to understand what you were trying to say by the end of your post? Did the reader learn something from your post, or feel that it held some value? It's okay if the answer is no to any of those questions. Some people have a natural talent when it comes to writing, and even more do not. But the good news is that those who don't can learn.

Before you can start searching for resources to improve your writing, you need to make an honest assessment of your skill level. Was high school English a struggle for you? Is smoke emanating from the autocorrect on your cell phone? Has it been a really long time since you've written a paragraph about anything? If the answer to these questions is yes, then you may want to take a look at a free or inexpensive online basic writing course. Udemy has some great online classes that range from basic grammar to blog-specific writing.

If you're able to attend a class in person, check out your local community college. Many offer reduced-cost non-credit classes in creative and other types of writing. You may also want to take a look at writing groups in your local community using the MeetUp app or a Facebook group. Many offer regular workshops where budding writers can critique each other's work and brainstorm ideas for new stories.

Just keep in mind that if your goal is to be taken seriously as a writer, and eventually to monetize your blog by partnering with brands or advertisers, your writing needs to be solid. However, if you're just getting started, don't stress out about making your posts perfect right away. Begin like you're writing an email to a friend. After a while, start running your posts through Grammarly with the settings on "casual" and "informal." Pay attention to the suggestions the site offers for correctness and clarity, and that will help you avoid the making the same mistakes in the future.

Choosing post topics

There are a few guidelines I like to follow when deciding what I want to write about for my blog. Before I even choose a specific topic, I have to decide what my goal is for each post. Do I need to write about the accessibility of a destination I just returned from? Did some new information emerge about accessible travel I need to educate others about? Are my blog views in a slump, meaning I need to write something that will cause a spike in traffic?

You also need to figure out who you're writing for; this is called your target audience. Ultimately, you want to write something that your existing audience will love, but something that will also help attract new readers. Picking good topics encourages your readers to share your content with others (I'll discuss this in more detail in Chapter 6). This is why you constantly need to ask yourself, *What do my readers want?* If you're a new blogger, you need to find out the interests of your potential audience.

A great way to do this is to join and be active in Facebook groups and online forums relevant to your blog topic. What do people in those groups talk about? What questions are they asking over and over? More importantly, where are the gaps in knowledge that you can fill? This is how you provide value by picking the right blog post topics.

However, the most important guideline I follow when picking post topics is to *always be authentic.* It's okay to share someone else's knowledge or experience, but it should serve as an example and not the focus of your post. Write about things you've done, places you've been, conversations you've shared, and feelings you've had. People will read your writing and start following your work if they feel connected to you based on shared experience. They will then be more inclined to follow your advice or recommendations as an authority. Authenticity is how you earn your readers' trust.

Choosing post titles

I'll be the first person to admit that I'm terrible at creating titles for articles. How do you sum up the content of a 2,000-word blog post in ten words or less? I've struggled with this for years, but blogging has helped me improve. First, you should know why a blog post title is so important.

Think about the last Google search you did. Think about the words you typed in the search bar, what the results showed, and which result(s) you clicked on. Chances are, you clicked on the link that most closely resembled your search terms. This is the foundation of something called search engine optimization (SEO), which I'll discuss in Chapter 5. You want your post titles to not only accurately reflect what your blog post is about, but you want the title to answer your readers' questions about your post's topic.

Structuring your posts

Writing a blog post is different than writing a school paper, a report for work, or even in a notebook. While the writing style is typically different, the basic structure of many blog posts resembles a newspaper article. Most paragraphs are short, so there are more of them. More people read blogs on mobile devices than on computer screens. This means that text blocks take up more space on smaller screens. It's easier for our brains to process ideas when there are breaks in the text rather than a huge monolithic rectangle filling a whole screen with words.

Using sub-headers in your posts helps your readers identify distinct ideas or points. You can accomplish the same thing with bullet points or numbered lists. However, I recommend using these sparingly, as they can break up the flow of a post. Ideally, your posts should contain more paragraphs and smoothly flowing text that bullet points or short lists.

Integrating media

One of the best ways to make your blog posts more interesting is to incorporate media. This could include photos, videos, diagrams, or even cartoons. The media you choose will depend on your post topic. If you decide to write about travel, then it's a good idea to scatter some travel photos and a few videos between paragraphs. If you're writing about different ways to exercise in a wheelchair, include instructive photos of various positions. If you're teaching people how to code, embed some screenshots so people can make the visual connection.

Many people don't feel comfortable in front of a camera, and this may well be the case even more frequently in the disability community. For years, I posted travel photos on Instagram that were nice, but could have been taken by anyone in that exact spot. When I decided to start appearing in my photos by using a travel tripod with a remote shutter, my likes and comments (i.e., engagement rate) skyrocketed. Why? Because people were able to make a connection with someone like them, clearly doing something they could picture themselves doing.

If you don't have any personal photos relevant to a post, don't be afraid to use stock photography from sites like Pixabay. The most important thing to remember when using photos that are not yours is to avoid copyright infringement at all costs. For this, I like to use Wikimedia Commons for royalty-free image searches. Always remember that anytime you use a photo in a blog post that you found on the Internet, there's a really good chance you are violating someone's copyright, and you could be held legally liable.

Think about how you can make a visual connection with your blog readers. Yes, this may require you to step outside your comfort zone.

However, we're living in a virtual world where our readers can be thousands of miles away. I've been lucky enough to meet many of my blog readers, but you may not. Letting them see you and hear you, especially doing things they hope to do someday, is the best way to connect with people through your blog. You can make this happen with a solid media integration plan.

5 HELPING PEOPLE FIND YOUR BLOG

What good is going through all the trouble of creating a great blog if nobody knows it exists? It's not enough just to rely on a Google search for the subject of your blog to direct potential readers to your website. There are over 600 million blogs on the Internet right now, and that number is growing every day. That means a lot of work must go into making your blog easy to find among all that competition. Fortunately, there are plenty of resources out there to help you make that happen.

What is SEO?

SEO is an acronym for "search engine optimization." Simply put, SEO is the practice of setting up your blog so it's as easy as possible for people to find using an Internet search engine. Some good SEO practices are simple and easy to implement; those are the ones I'll be focusing on in this chapter. Others are more complex and time-consuming, and I will suggest some excellent resources so you can learn more from the real SEO experts.

The ultimate goal of having good SEO on your blog is to appear on the first page of Google (or another search engine) results after someone uses search terms related to one of your blog posts. For example, if you type *wheelchair accessible Dublin* in the Google search bar, my blog post is the first result you'll see. This happens due to a combination of factors. But most importantly, I've written a post that provides value because it contains information many people are looking for.

Write content that people look for

How do you discover what people want to know? You're not a mind reader, so this may seem like a difficult prospect at first. Fortunately, there are several ways to give potential readers exactly what they want.

First, ask yourself what *you* wanted to know when you first got involved in the topic of your blog. Let's say you write about your life with a specific chronic illness, and you were diagnosed as a young adult. What questions did you have? What do you know now that you wish you had known then? What tips or "life hacks" can you provide people with your condition to make life easier? What's the latest news in research and treatment? These are some ways you can provide valuable content for readers.

Another way to find out what type of information people want is to join Facebook groups related to your blog topic. For example, let's say you have a service dog—specifically, a golden retriever—and you write about life with a service dog. You can join Facebook groups about service dogs, or golden retrievers, or even start your own Facebook group about having a golden retriever service dog. Pay attention to what people are asking and discussing.

Some of my peers say I pay too much attention to what my competition is doing, and that I should just "do me" and focus on my own blog. As a marketing major with an undergraduate business degree, I think that's terrible advice. Every business, from international conglomerate to small mom-and-pop store, knows what their competition is up to. I watch my competitors for several reasons: first, to see what they're doing so I can do it better; second, to see what they're *not* doing so I can start; and third, to keep me motivated so I don't fall behind the curve.

Don't be discouraged from starting a blog about Disneyland just because there are a bunch of them already out there. The key in a high-competition niche is to write content that people want, but not too many bloggers are offering. I'm an accessible travel blogger, and there are several of us out there. There are some destinations or topics many of us have written about, but usually each perspective is a bit different. I've been to some places where my competitors have not, which helps. Find something unique about Disneyland that other bloggers haven't written about that your specific audience will love.

Learn what keywords are and how to use them

Dictionary.com defines a keyword as "a word or concept of great significance." In the context of blogging, keywords are the little golden nuggets that potential readers are searching for on the Internet. The magic question of SEO is, *How do I know what keywords to use, and what do I do with them?*

First, your keywords are going to be different for every blog post. If you're writing a post designed to bring traffic to your blog (which is ideal if you want to make money), you should write it in a way that focuses on these keywords. They should be the most frequently used terms in Google searches on a particular topic.

Let's use one of my most popular blog posts as an example. My readers love it when I publish anything about wheelchair accessible beaches, especially those in Florida. I also know that a lot of people are searching the Internet for resources about accessible beaches in Florida. I know this a few different ways. First, those posts have some of the highest hit counts on my blog. Second, the plug-ins and websites I use with my blog help me keep track of statistics tell me some of the most common search terms used to find my blog (more on tracking and measuring in Chapter 8).

Third, there are various services available to help you do keyword research. These are services that help you find the most common words and phrases used in Internet searches to find articles related to things you can write about. In my blog post example, the most prominent keywords are *wheelchair, accessible, beaches,* and *Florida.* It's up to me to use the results of my keyword research to figure out exactly how to write the title of my blog post so it appears as close to the top of the search engine results page (SERP) as possible.

For example, you would be unwise to just write "visit Florida beaches." It's better to write "visit accessible Fkorida beaches," but best to write "visit accessible Florida beaches in a wheelchair." These phrases are known as longtail keywords. The more you use a key phrase throughout your blog post (including the title), the higher up your post will appear in search engine results when people type the phrase into Google.

Two of the more popular keyword search services are Keysearch and SEMrush. Keysearch has a free option, and while SEMrush is considered the gold standard, it's also very expensive. I would only recommend it for advanced bloggers with already decent traffic. Google also has a free keyword planner, but you have to create a Google Ads account to use it.

I used Keysearch for several months, but found it to be of limited utility for wheelchair or disability-related blog posts. The volume of searches was just too low for the service to be effective. I have a much easier time determining what my audience wants by examining my traffic for existing blog posts, as well as being an active participant in Facebook groups with thousands of wheelchair travelers. I highly recommend joining Facebook groups related to your blog's topic and paying attention to the types of questions that members are asking.

Ultimately, the biggest decision you have to make when it comes to using keywords in your blog posts is whether to write for your audience or write for yourself. If your goal is to land as many eyeballs as possible on a blog post, then find out how to answer the questions that most people are asking about your blog's topic. Using keywords carefully selected from these questions in your post title and sprinkled throughout your post will help search engines—and thus potential readers—find you.

You can never write too much…or can you?

It's totally up to you how long or short you want your blog post to be. However, for SEO purposes, your posts should never be shorter than 300 words. Ideally, they should be between 500-700 words, but there's also an argument to be made for why they should be even longer.

People searching for specific answers to their questions don't usually want to spend a lot of time digging through a blog post to find those answers. However, if your post intends to offer a wide variety of options for something that requires a more detailed explanation, then a longer post would be more appropriate.

One way to determine what a good length for your blog post might be is to conduct a SERP analysis. Let's say you want to write a blog post about upper body exercises you can perform in a wheelchair. Do a Google search for [upper body exercises wheelchair], and check out the results on page one. Do a word count of the top ten blog posts or articles, and see if you notice a pattern. Or, you can do a qualitative check. Which post or article best answers the inquiry, and why? And how many words did it require to do that?

It's a fine line to walk when deciding on the length of a blog post because you don't want to bore your audience, but you do want to keep readers on your website as long as possible. One way to do this is with long posts (3,000 words or more) filled with great keywords and awesome content. More text means more keywords that will help people find your post, and great content will keep visitors reading. You can break up longer posts into more digestible sections using headers and sub-headers, photos, and bullet points.

Have a good linking strategy

Embedding hyperlinks in your blog posts is an essential component of your overall SEO strategy. There are three different types of links that bloggers use, and each serves a different purpose: internal links, external links, and inbound links.

In addition to keeping readers on your website for extended periods, you also want them to visit more than just one page. This lowers something called your bounce rate, which measures the behavior of your blog visitors—specifically, how much of your site they see before they go elsewhere, or "bounce." A lower bounce rate means that when people visit one page or post on your site, they tend to visit other pages or posts on your site during their session. A lower bounce rate usually signals that your entire website is appealing, beyond just one blog post.

You can encourage visitors to your blog to look around by making it easy for them to read other posts on your site. The best way to do this is through internal linking. However, this won't be possible until you've written several blog posts, ideally quite a few that are somehow related to one another. That's okay because it gives you an excuse to write more content! All you have to do when writing a blog post is to embed a link to another one of your blog posts, ideally one that is directly related to the text you've highlighted for the link.

For example, a couple of years ago, I wrote a blog post on how wheelchair users can use trains in Europe. I've used trains all over the continent, and I noted examples from Amsterdam, Vienna, and Munich. Since I have visited these cities individually and written blog posts about them, in my post about trains, I highlighted those cities with an internal link to each city post. In another example, I wrote a post about the best wheelchair accessible vacation spots in Florida. Two of my selections were Orlando and Miami, which allowed me to link internally to my blog posts about wheelchair accessible things to do in each of those cities. Doing this also demonstrate to Google that I have authority on the topic because I've written other blog posts that are related.

Another thing you want is referrals to your blog from other websites. This happens when another blog or website embeds a link to your blog in a post or on their page. This is called an inbound link, and some people would say you can't have enough of them. It can be hard to come by good quality inbound links, but fortunately there are some good strategies for how to obtain them (more about this in Chapter 7).

The third type of link you will use in your blog posts is an external link, which is simply a link to another website. It may seem counterintuitive to include a link in your blog post that will take readers to another site when you want to keep them on your site as possible. However, there is a benefit to this.

Linking to trustworthy and informative links in your blog posts helps you build credibility with your readers. It can also help you build the authority of your website (more about this in Chapter 7). Yes, there's always a risk that it will take readers away from your site. However, this is part of the value that you offer your readers.

For example, if I'm writing a blog post about ten accessible things to do in San Diego, I will write about at least one museum. Chances are that museum will have a website with a page containing information about the museum's wheelchair accessibility. In the paragraph where I write about the museum, I will include an external link to that specific accessibility page. Can I cut and paste all of that information into my paragraph? Sure. But through external linking, my blog readers know I'm aware of exactly where to find the information they need. It also keeps my blog post more concise, with fewer boring technical details.

Take your time with meta descriptions and URLs

When you conduct a Google search for a topic, the results page features a ranked list of websites. Each result will have a hyperlinked web page title highlighted in blue. Below that, you will likely see two lines of a very brief summary that give you an idea of the information on that page. This is the meta description for a website or blog post. When you use a blog platform like WordPress to create posts, you have the option at the bottom of the text box to write a brief meta description for the post. You also have the option to create a custom URL for that post instead of the one automatically generated by WordPress.

These little snippets of text may not seem like a big deal, but SEO encompasses pretty much anything and everything where words are involved on your blog. When writing out your meta descriptions for posts, the URL, and even the descriptions for your images, use keywords whenever possible. Google sees all, and the more it sees your keywords on your post page, the more it believes your post is relevant to the person conducting a search using those keywords.

One thing I wish I had known when I first started blogging was that I shouldn't include dates in my post URLs. WordPress will do this automatically, but you can go into your WordPress settings to choose the format you want as the default for your post URLs. Make sure you pick one that does not include the date.

Use the Yoast plug-in as a guide

One of the most commonly used WordPress plug-ins is called Yoast. It measures the level of SEO for each one of your blog posts using a stoplight system. You can use Yoast for free, but I highly recommend paying the $99 per year for the full spectrum of services. It's completely integrated into your post editor, and will give you a red/yellow/green rating for things like the length of your post, whether or not you have outgoing and internal links, and whether or not you have images in your post.

Some people think they have to live or die by the Yoast stoplight, and that's just not true. You do not have to have everything showing green for your post to be good to go on SEO. The plug-in is there just to help remind you of things to include in your posts where you can improve your SEO. Can you write a longer post, include more pictures, and add a few more outbound links? Then do so if those items are showing up as red or orange. Not enough alt attributes for your images? You'll be okay.

For more details on how to dramatically (and easily) improve the SEO on your blog, I highly recommend investing in SEO The Easy Way, *a course by Gemma and Laura at Make Traffic Happen. It's an easy to understand step-by-step guide to take your blog to the next level of competitiveness.*

6 SPREADING THE WORD

In Chapter 5, I spoke about ways to make your blog easier to find through Google searches. Ultimately, that's a passive way of increasing traffic to your blog. In this chapter, I want to talk about proactive measures you can take to make sure the right people know about your blog.

Establish your brand

A brand is defined as an identifying symbol, mark, logo, or word that companies use to distinguish their product or service from others. When you hear McDonald's, you think of those golden arches. When you hear Apple, you think of that crisp fruit image on the back of your iPhone. While these logos are good tangible examples of corporate brands, people can have brands, too.

Technically speaking, my company, Spin the Globe, has a logo. I commissioned a graphic artist friend of mine to create the design. I gave him the line art for a more modern and forward-leaning wheelchair user, and told him I wanted to incorporate the elements of travel and femininity. I was thrilled with the results, and two years later I got it registered as a legal trademark. This is my visual brand.

However, I also represent a more nuanced brand—wheelchair accessible travel. To go even further than that, I represent women traveling solo in wheelchairs. While there is no direct reference in my logo to these concepts in words, the combination of the graphic and the images on my blog makes it clear that this is my brand. My professional goal is always this: When people hear *wheelchair accessible travel*, I want them to picture my logo and think of me, and ultimately my blog.

Establishing your personal brand involves some decisions. What words or phrases or concepts do you want people to associate with you? How can you convey that into a simple and eye-catching logo or image? How can you differentiate yourself as a brand from your competition? The good news is that it's pretty easy to create a logo these days. Even if you have absolutely zero artistic talent, you can go to a website like Fiverr and work with a freelance graphic artist to create a logo for you at a very low cost. Better yet, hit up one of your more artistic friends who has some skill with PowerPoint or Photoshop to draw something up for you.

One piece of advice that I will give you with regards to a brand—once you choose it, stick with it. Huge corporations go through the rebranding process every so often to stay relevant and modern. However, it can be a time-consuming, expensive, and confusing process. It takes time to build up brand recognition and reputation, so the last thing you want to do is potentially squander all of that because you didn't like your logo to begin with.

You also want to pick something that can grow with you. If you include the number of dogs you have in your blog name, what happens if you get another dog? If you include the specific brand of wheelchair you use, what happens if you get a new wheelchair from a different brand? If you include your location, what happens if you move? Take your time at the start to find something you really love, and commit to it.

Create a press kit

A press kit will be a vital part of your marketing arsenal when it comes time to monetize your blog. This means that your blog is relatively well known in your topic's community, you have social media followers in the thousands, and you are getting at least 10,000 monthly page views. It is a résumé of sorts, but designed to be visually appealing and to put forth your best qualities as a blogger. You can create either a hard copy press kit or a digital version (or both), and each has its pros and cons. Which one you decide to create depends largely on how you plan to use it.

There is some necessary information that all press kits should contain. Ideally, it should only be two pages long – front and back of a single sheet of paper. If it's a digital kit, you have more freedom to include additional photos and data without being limited to hard copy sheets. You should include a summary of who you are and what you write about. Potential partners will want to know your blog reader demographics, as well as your page view statistics and social media follower counts. If you Google the phrase *press kit example*, you'll get some great ideas for layouts. If you don't think you have the skills to make one yourself, this is something else you can outsource to a freelancer on Fiverr or Upwork.

I created my first press kit on paper because I was mainly using it during travel writing conferences. I needed something tangible to provide tourism boards, and it served as a conversation piece where I could point to specific skills I wanted to emphasize. However, now I rely exclusively on my digital media kit.

A hard copy media kit, while easy to create on PowerPoint or Word, can be expensive and time-consuming to print. Also, because your traffic stats and follower accounts will frequently change, you have to update and print out an entire new set with each update. That being said, they are easy to hand out on short notice, and it's easier for recipients to remember who you are without you having to remind them in an email first.

I prefer digital media kits because they are super easy to create using software like Adobe Spark, and it's so much easier to send a link rather than a large attachment of your hard copy digital file. If you are cold pitching a company to propose a collaboration, you also may not have the option of sending your media kit as a file. It's much easier to share a link to your digital kit, especially if the submission has to be made using an online contact form rather than an email.

Make the most of social media

There is a very good chance that you learned about this book through social media. It's my number one marketing lifeline for absolutely everything I produce, from blog posts and books to photos and videos. If you're not already familiar with the various social media sharing platforms, it can seem very intimidating. Fortunately, the learning curve is pretty small, and you have a wide variety of social options depending on what you need. Here is a sample of different major social media platforms you can use to spread the word about your blog.

Facebook. This is my personal favorite because I believe it's the most versatile. I can post my travel photos, travel videos, I can do live streaming from my destinations, or I can just share funny memes. Every time I publish a new blog post, I post a short description and a link on Facebook when most of my readers will be online. You can pay to boost the reach of your posts, although Facebook has become very stingy in this regard in the past year by increasing the required payment to reach the same number of people. The biggest downside is that it's almost impossible to monetize any Facebook posts that might go viral. However, it's the number one traffic generator to my blog outside of Google searches.

I always encourage bloggers to join Facebook groups related to their blog topic. It's a great way to learn about the latest trends and information gaps in your field. In some groups, it's also possible to share links to your blog posts. Just be very careful when reading the group rules so that you don't violate any self-promotion restrictions. Another thing I like to do is find the Facebook pages for companies or destinations that I (positively) mention in my blog posts. Then I contact them through Facebook Messenger, asking them to share my post with their followers through their social media channels. They don't always agree, but when they do, you could gain exposure of your blog to potentially hundreds of thousands of people.

Instagram. Many bloggers these days have a love/hate relationship with Instagram. This is the number one place to post any photos you take in conjunction with your blog. Years ago, your photos would be shown to your followers chronologically, but Instagram has updated their algorithm several times to prioritize photos with greater likes and engagement. Engagement overall on the platform has declined, and it's harder than ever to gain new followers. It also typically generates very little traffic to blogs. Still, you need to have a well-populated Instagram account to attract the interest of brands you may want to work with. Take and post photos of absolutely anything and everything related to your blog, and be sure to follow the accounts of other Instagrammers in your same subject area.

Twitter. I'll be the first one to tell you that I can't stand Twitter. Your messages (known as tweets) are limited to 280 characters or less, although you can post links, photos, and videos under two minutes long. Because of algorithm changes in the last couple of years, it's incredibly challenging to gain new Twitter followers unless one of your tweets happens to go viral. Still, it's a necessity, and I post a link to all of my blog posts as soon as they're published. I will say that Twitter is a good place to post short, personal, funny thoughts, and you can gain some followers by using a trending hashtag if it relates to your content. Make sure to follow other Twitter users in your subject area, and there's a good chance they will follow you back.

YouTube. These days, video is an essential component to almost every type of blog out there. Video isn't just a way for your readers and followers to learn about your blog topic. It's a way for them to connect to you as a person. Not everyone is comfortable being recorded for videos, and this isn't a requirement for all bloggers. However, YouTube is also a type of search engine just like Google. If you make and post videos about things directly related to your blog, you can use detailed descriptions that are searchable. Your videos don't have to look professionally produced, either. YouTube is also a platform that can potentially be monetized if you gain enough subscribers.

Pinterest. The easiest way to describe Pinterest is to say it's like a huge bulletin board. You create pins, which are more or less pretty graphics with photos that link to your blog posts. You then post these pins to different virtual boards that you create for different categories. For example, I have a board for accessible travel, one for technology, and one for inspirational quotes. You can post pins to your boards that you create, or pins that you're sharing from other people's boards. Pinterest is also searchable like Google, so it's important to use detailed descriptions and hashtags when you post your pins so that people can find you. The platform sends a few dozen referrals to my travel blog every month. However, it's a gold mine of traffic for blogs about parenting, gardening, fashion, arts and crafts, and food.

For some fantastic and detailed information on branding and making the most of social media as a new blogger, check out Branding Yourself *by Erik Deckers.*

Create an email list

Email lists work differently for bloggers depending on your subject matter and community. I highly recommend that all bloggers have a pop-up or subscription box on their site where readers can sign-up for emails (there are plug-ins for that). This means that they will automatically get notified every time you publish something new. This also means you can harvest your email list and use it for promotional purposes.

Contacting your blog readers by email is tricky. You don't want to miss out on opportunities to inform them about cool things you're doing or new products you're selling, but you also don't want them to get so sick of your emails that they unsubscribe. Some bloggers publish regular newsletters, and you should make sure your email subscribers know they're signing up to regularly receive the newsletter by email.

I will be the first to admit that I don't use my email list as effectively as I could. I have a combined total of roughly 4,000 people signed up, which means that I have a direct line to their eyeballs—as long as I can get them to open the email. There are many services you can use to send out mass emails to your list. Depending on how many people are on it, services can be free or charge a monthly fee. I use Mailchimp, but there are other services out there as well.

The best way to use your email list effectively is to decide early on what you want to do with it. I make full use of my email list whenever I publish a new book or organize a group cruise, for example. You can embed hyperlinks in your emails that will take readers to your eCommerce page, or a specific page on your blog, or a listing on Amazon. The most important thing is to create a subject line that will entice your recipients to actually open the email and read it. There are several articles available on the Internet that can help you with this; just Google *best email subject lines.*

Guest posts and collaborations

One of the best ways to get your name out there in your blog topic's community is to contribute a guest post to a related blog. No, you won't get paid. However, especially as a new blogger, you will reap several rewards from this. First, you are helping out a more established blogger by providing them with free content for their readers. Second, you are exposing your name and your writing to an established audience that is already interested in your blog's topic. Third, the hope is that the blog owner will provide a link to your blog, helping improve your domain authority (DA).

Domain authority is a search engine ranking score developed by a company called Moz, and it's designed to help predict how well a website will perform during a Google search. The score goes from 0 to 100, with 0 being a website that will rarely, if ever, show up in any search for any term, and 100 meaning the website is most likely to almost always appear in the number one results spot. Examples of websites in the upper 90s include the *New York Times* and major corporations like Apple or Ford Motor Company.

Your blog DA gets calculated using many factors. However, the one that you have the most control over is inbound links to your blog. The more links you have to your blog from websites with higher DA than yours, the bigger boost they provide to your own DA. By pitching a guest post or a collaboration to a popular blog in your area of expertise, and of course requesting a link back to your blog in exchange, they will pass on their "link juice" to you. You will also be providing an avenue to your blog for new readers.

Freelance writing

Getting published in an established newspaper, magazine, or website can be a gold mine for both publicity and link juice. The kicker to landing this kind of writing gig is that you have to be *really* good writer, and also have an established reputation as an expert—or at least someone with valuable experience—in whatever you're writing about. It also takes a specific skill set to pitch editors effectively with the idea for your article. Before you consider going down this route, make sure you have a well-populated blog with at least twenty posts of high-quality writing.

The best way to begin using freelance writing as a way to promote your blog is to start small. I love to submit pitches for opinion pieces to newspapers. I've been published in both my local paper, the *Orlando Sentinel*, and the *New York Times*. I don't think I have to tell you which paper was the tougher nut to crack. However, in both cases I got a blog mention and a hyperlink. Do I really need to explain how much link juice that *Times* piece provided for my domain authority?

It should come as no surprise that freelance writing typically doesn't pay very well. For the purposes of this book, I am encouraging it primarily as a way for you to get your name out there and promote your blog. However, you never know who is going to read your work. One avenue I would recommend is Help a Reporter Out, or HARO. This is a website and email subscription service where reporters across all fields seek input and articles from experts on a variety of subjects. They may be seeking an interview subject, or a full article. Even if one freelance piece only gets you $40, down the road you may snag a more lucrative and regular writing gig.

Public speaking, interviews, and podcasts

Once you've established yourself as an expert on your blog topic, it's time to put yourself out there—based on your level of comfort—with the media. I love public speaking and any sort of speaking engagement, but I am fully aware that many people fear being on stage more than they fear death. Given that this book is about blogging from your wheelchair (and most likely from home), radio interviews, Skype interviews, and podcasts are great ways to promote your writing without leaving home.

Public speaking engagements can be challenging to land, especially if you're looking for one to pay you enough money to make it worth the effort to appear. I have paid out of pocket for plenty of public speaking opportunities, but only because I thought the professional benefit and the exposure would be beneficial enough to warrant the cost. I have also spoken for free in my local community because it was more important to me to share my message then it was to make any money.

If you are new to public speaking, I would recommend starting small. Look for opportunities in your local community to share your blog's message. There are groups and meetups for every topic under the sun, and speaking to a small local group that gathers every month would be a great way for you to start. Local nursing homes, rehab facilities, Centers for Independent Living, or any other organization that caters to people with disabilities or wheelchair users love to have guest speakers with a positive message to share. I recently spoke to a small group of roughly sixty wheelchair users, their family members, and their caregivers at a rehab facility here in Florida. I sold all ten copies of my book on accessible cruising before I even opened my mouth.

If this still scares you to pieces, and you have the physical ability to speak clearly, I would highly recommend pitching your local radio station, or reaching out to a podcast producer. There are hundreds, if not thousands, of different podcasts out there, and their hosts are always looking for interesting guests. I love radio shows and podcasts because they're less of an interview and more like a conversation. You can speak for longer periods of time, and they love to promote whatever you want.

7 MAKING MONEY FROM YOUR BLOG

Make no mistake; getting to the point where you can make money from blogging is an investment. Just like writing a book, nobody starts to blog to get rich. However, just like authors, there are plenty of bloggers out there who make a full-time living from different income streams directly tied to their blogs. There are no shortcuts or get-rich-quick schemes. However, if this is your ultimate goal, here is some helpful information to set you on that path.

Create your business

Once you decide to start making money from your blog or writing in general, the smart thing to do is to create a business. There are many resources out there to help you decide what type of business to start, and your local city or county governments are great places for this. I have a sole proprietorship for my blog and travel agency. Maybe eventually I will convert it to a limited liability corporation (LLC), but for now, this works for me. The great thing about sole proprietorships is that they are easy and inexpensive to start. Make sure you check with your city, county, and state for any licenses or business tax receipts you have to apply for in order to create your business.

After you've gone through the steps to create your business, you still have a few logistics to handle. First, I recommend establishing a separate bank account for your business income, as this will make tax time a lot easier. Second, if you haven't done so already, create social media accounts for your blog separate from your personal accounts. Third, if you plan on coming into contact with anyone who can benefit from the information your blog, you'll want to create some business cards. You can always get some great discounts on good quality business cards at Vistaprint, which is what I use for all my promotional materials.

Finally, if you have the physical ability to leave the house, consider joining the local Chamber of Commerce. Their meetings are great opportunities for networking, and it's also a fantastic way for you to increase the representation of wheelchair users in the business community. I love to mix and mingle with other small business owners because it helps people realize that we can work and contribute just as much as anyone else. It's also a fun way to make new friends.

Affiliate programs

One way to generate some income through your blog is to work with affiliates. These are companies that provide you with images or links to post on your blog that connect to their products. If one of your readers clicks on those images or links and purchases one of their products or services, you then earn a percentage of the purchase price. Let's say that you run a blog about model cars. You may want to partner up with a company that sells model car paint. They can provide you with a link to their online shop, and when one of your readers buys a paint set, the company will then give you 10 percent of what that customer paid for the set.

Another way to earn affiliate income is to apply to large affiliate programs. One of the most popular and easy to use is Amazon. About a year ago, I wrote a blog post about tools and gadgets that make life easier for wheelchair users at home. After every paragraph describing each item, I posted a link provided by my affiliate program to that gadget's listing on Amazon's website. If my readers click on that link, I make a percentage of anything they buy during that particular visit to Amazon, whether it's the item I described or something else that's completely unrelated.

Digital advertising

Another common way to earn income through your blog is through digital advertising networks. There are several out there, but some are more trouble than they're worth because you won't make any real money until you have at least 10,000 page views per month. Many bloggers with lower monthly page view counts like to start with Google AdSense. This service posts ads on your site that are relevant to your content. You have to be able to make certain spaces available on your blog for Google's ads, so you may have to modify your theme to accommodate this. Google AdSense also doesn't pay very well, but it's open to bloggers who don't have a lot of traffic.

Once you reach over 10,000 views, there are other more lucrative advertising platforms you can apply to, like Ezoic. It pays better than Google AdSense, but it requires you to mess around with the script for your theme, and many users complain that it can slow down your blog performance. The Holy Grail for digital advertising is Mediavine. Advertisers pay Mediavine bloggers generously, and they are incredibly easy to use and work with.

However, Mediavine also has strict traffic requirements for membership. You can't apply until you have at least 25,000 monthly *sessions*, which usually equates to about 35,000 monthly page views. It's also important for a majority of your blog traffic to come from the United States and other English-speaking countries. However, it's totally worth the hustle to get to that point, as you can start making a few hundred dollars every month right out of the gate. Mediavine members with a million monthly page views per month or more can make six figures in advertising revenue alone (remember the poultry lady?).

If you're just starting out with digital ads and you have a lower number of monthly page views, you may be tempted to saturate your blog with more ads to make more money. This is dangerous because it can negatively affect your reader experience enough to turn them off from your blog altogether. It's a constant and delicate balancing act for any blogger who wants to earn advertising income. Just keep paying attention to your traffic statistics and the loading time for your blog pages after you implement any new advertising program.

Sponsored posts and ads

I will be perfectly honest and tell you that sponsored posts and ads are tricky territory. This is where you work directly with a company that pays you to place their ads on your blog, or to write about their products for a fee. The more monthly page views you have, the more you can charge. While it might be tempting to write about or advertise for anyone who will pay you something, that can come with a considerable cost—your integrity as a blogger, and subsequently the faith of your audience.

I am entirely completely open to sponsored posts and ads, and have been approached dozens of times by companies requesting them. However, I have had to turn most of them down because they want me to write about or advertise products I wouldn't personally use, or products that my wheelchair-using audience would never use. I have written blog posts about products that have been provided to me for free to review, and for both ethical and legal reasons, I have to clearly state that fact in my blog post. The last thing I want to do is encourage my blog readers to buy something I think is total garbage.

The biggest ethical dilemma when it comes to sponsored posts and ads is the requirement for you to be honest about those products or services. If the company is paying you several hundred dollars to write about their widget, you can imagine they're not going to be happy if you write a blog post saying the widget was useless or hard to use. So, what do you do if the product or service sucks?

Obviously, this is a personal decision. It can be like threading a needle, but I use the clichéd sandwich or Oreo feedback approach (positive-negative-positive). I introduce the product or service and explain what it's supposed to do and who it's supposed to benefit. I lay out the pros at the beginning, then honestly explain all the cons. At the end, whenever possible, I say that the product or service may not work for certain people, but might benefit others. I also try to be as specific as possible regarding whom it will help and whom it won't. I also do my research about the product or service being offered before replying to the request, and I never accept a request to review something I can't be positive about at all.

As a travel blogger, I am sometimes provided with complimentary tours and transportation and hotel stays by destinations that want me to write about their wheelchair accessibility. Before I accept, I always tell them upfront that it's my duty to be honest with my readers because we're not just talking about wheelchair travelers potentially losing money for that experience; we're talking about personal safety. Fortunately, on the few occasions where I have had to critique the lack of accessibility on a press trip, my hosts have used it as a way to improve accessibility for future visitors. Hopefully, if you get the opportunity to create a sponsored review, your sponsor will use any critique to improve their product.

ECommerce

Making stuff and selling stuff online is the name of the game with eCommerce! This is simply how you sell merchandise directly from your blog. One of the great things about using WordPress is that there are plug-ins available (I use WooCommerce) that create an entire online shop for your theme, as long as your theme is compatible with eCommerce. I have a simple online shop for my travel blog. I create items like T-shirts with fun sayings and lighthearted magnets designed for wheelchair vans. Because I outsource them for delivery on demand, I don't have to worry about maintaining any inventory in my house. It doesn't cost me anything to have that online shop, and I make a quick little profit anytime someone orders an item.

Not every blog is about a topic that lends itself to merchandise, which is why it's great to have a logo you can use to promote your brand. It's super easy to create promotional materials on Vistaprint with your logo, like shirts, mugs, keychains, and water bottles. You can use WooCommerce to accept orders and payment, then fulfill the order through your supplier. However, if you have the potential to create absolutely anything that you can sell and ship, creating an online shop through your blog is a must!

8 HOW TO MEASURE SUCCESS AND SET GOALS

After spending countless hours and days and weeks and months crafting a genuinely outstanding blog, how will you know if you're actually succeeding, or even coming close to reaching your goals? Fortunately, there are many ways to measure progress and success in the blogging world. Statistics are *everything* when it comes to successful blogging, both for creating new business relationships and for making more money. Here are the main tools you should be using and the most important numbers you should be examining to track your progress.

Google Analytics

I will warn you that the first time you use Google Analytics (GA), it will probably make your head explode. However, this is the most important tool you will ever use to measure anything important regarding your blog's performance, including things like page views, sessions, unique visitors, and your bounce rate. The first thing you have to do to take advantage of Google Analytics is to embed what's called a GA code into the script for your blog.

To do this, you first have to register your blog with Google Analytics. Google provides easy-to-follow instructions after this on how to get this

GA code. Then you can use a Google Analytics plug-in through WordPress to automatically embed that tracking code into your theme. This tracking code is what records every interaction with your blog on the Internet. *Be VERY careful not to install the GA code twice*! This will give you inaccurate page view counts and drop your bounce rate close to zero.

After you set up Google Analytics, you need to be patient. After about three months of recording your traffic, you'll start to see the first useful data. In addition to showing you your blog's daily traffic, eventually it can tell you what search terms people are using to reach your blog, what countries your blog traffic is coming from, and the demographics of your blog audience. By understanding the data that GA provides, you can improve your blog's performance by tailoring your content to better meet the needs of your audience.

Follower counts

This is easily one of the most controversial and highly debated topics among bloggers today. The standard practice—and bloodsport, if I'm perfectly honest—has historically been to accumulate as many followers as possible across all your social media platforms. Entire books have been written about how to increase your social media follower count. Shady businesses around the world make tons of money selling thousands of fake followers to desperate bloggers who risk getting their accounts blacklisted just to have bigger numbers. But why are these follower counts so important?

To really answer this, first it's crucial to understand how social media following works. If you are a Facebook user and you visit a business page (e.g., Ferrari), you have the option to like that business by clicking on the thumbs-up symbol next to the business name. BOOM! You're a follower of Ferrari. Now, every time that Ferrari posts on Facebook, that post will appear in your personal Facebook feed. How often you see Ferrari's posts depends on how often you interact with them. If you like their posts and comment on them with some frequency, you will see their posts more often in your feed.

This algorithm tends to work the same way with Twitter and Instagram. If you follow a Twitter user, all of their tweets will automatically be added to your Twitter feed. However, the order in which you see tweets posted by the accounts you follow is not chronological. Your Instagram feed content is also highly dependent on your interaction through likes and comments. Please keep this in mind because it will be very important in the next section.

The reason why growing your follower count as much as possible is a big deal today is because that seems to be the standard by which brands measure your value as a partner. Most brands believe that the more followers you have, the more eyeballs will see whatever *you* post, and the more eyeballs will see *their* products and services if they work with you to promote them. Unfortunately for these companies and the millions of dollars they spend on influencer marketing, this often isn't the case. However, if you have a lower follower count because you're just getting started as a blogger, it's possible to use that to your advantage by cultivating a high engagement rate.

Engagement rates

The engagement rate is the percentage of your followers for a particular social media account that actively engages with your posts. This means that someone either likes or comments on your Instagram photo or your tweet or your Facebook post. Despite all the billions of social media followers out there in the world, overall social media engagement rates are ridiculously low. According to the social media analysis company Rival IQ, the average engagement rate in 2019 across all industries for Facebook was .09 percent; for Instagram it was 1.6 percent; and for Twitter it was .048 percent. This means that for every 10,000 posts on Facebook, only nine of them were receiving any likes or comments.

So how do you compete with social media accounts that have ten times or even a hundred times the number of followers you have? By raising your engagement rate. As I mentioned in the paragraph above, the average engagement rate for Facebook in 2019 was .09 percent. The engagement rate for my blog Facebook page was 16.1 percent—*nearly 180 times the industry average.* My Twitter engagement rate was 2 percent—*nearly 42 times the industry average.* These are things you can promote when pitching yourself to a brand. Unlike monthly traffic, it's really easy to calculate the engagement rates of your competitors. You'd be amazed at how tiny the engagement rates can be for social media accounts with millions of followers.

But to make this strategy work, you have to develop an engaged social media audience. It's not enough to just accept likes and comments, or to just post whatever you want on your social media pages. It's also not enough just to post your own content. Post articles related to your blog's topic that your audience will find valuable, educational, or just plain funny. Post cartoons and silly videos. Post viral memes that your audience will share or react to. You can even post things that make them angry (not towards you), which is relatively easy to do in the disability community where there is so much injustice to choose from.

Just post to make your followers feel something, which will encourage them to engage. *This* is how you demonstrate to brands and potential business partners that real eyeballs will land on their content.

APPENDIX A – GLOSSARY

Affiliate: A company that provides bloggers a percentage of sales generated through product or service links placed on their blogs.

Analytics: The measurement and analysis of website or blog performance.

Bounce Rate: A measure of blog visitor behavior—specifically, how much of a site they see before they go elsewhere, or "bounce."

Brand: An identifying symbol, mark, logo, or word that companies use to distinguish their product or service from others.

Domain: The name of a website, or what comes after the http://www.

Domain Authority: A search engine ranking score developed by a company called Moz, designed to help predict how well a website will perform during a Google search.

ECommerce: The practice of selling goods and services online.

Engagement Rate: The percentage of followers for a particular social media account that actively engages with posts through likes and comments.

Host: A company that provides a virtual place to park a domain name and a blog's website.

Keyword: A term(s) in a blog post that encapsulates its main idea(s).

Meta Description: A short summary of a web page's contents, usually shown on a search engine's results page.

Niche: A small corner, or very specific blogging topic or specialty.

Platform: The software and associated tools used to create a blog. Also known as a content management system (e.g., WordPress, SquareSpace, Wix)

Plug-in: A software component that allows easy customization of a blog or website.

Press Kit: A package of promotional material provided to members of the press or potential business partners. Can be hardcopy or digital.

Referral: When a website directs readers to another website using a hyperlink.

SEO: Search engine optimization. A system for configuring your blog and writing posts in a way that makes them easier to find during an Internet search.

SERP: Search engine results page. What you see after entering search terms into an engine like Google.

Template: A pre-set website or blog design that can be customized.

TLD: Top-level domain. Those three letters after the dot at the end of a website address (e.g., com, net, org)

URL: Universal resource locator. Basically, a website address.

WooCommerce: A plug-in that allows you to create an online shop and payment system integrated directly into your blog.

WordPress: A popular content management system that allows you to create a website or blog.

APPENDIX B – RESOURCES

While I have scattered links to various blogging resources throughout this book, I thought it would make sense to put them all together in one place for reference.

CH 3 – CREATING YOUR BLOG

Google domain search tool
Namecheckr (domain availability search tool)
Learn to Code with Me (what to look for in a good host)
WhoIsHostingThis? (site host comparison tool)
Make a Website (CMS platform comparison tool)
WordPress.org vs. WordPress.com

CH 4 – WRITING FOR YOUR BLOG

Udemy (online writing courses)
Pixabay (stock photos)
Wikimedia Commons (royalty-free photos)

CH 5 – HELPING PEOPLE FIND YOUR BLOG

SEO The Easy Way

CH 6 – SPREADING THE WORD

Branding Yourself
Help a Reporter Out (HARO)

CH 7 – MAKING MONEY FROM YOUR BLOG

SBA: 10 Steps to Start Your Business
WooCommerce (eCommerce plug-in documentation)

CH 8 – HOW TO MEASURE SUCCESS AND SET GOALS

Google Analytics registration instructions
Understanding Google Analytics

ABOUT THE AUTHOR

Sylvia Longmire is an accessible travel writer and photographer, travel agent, author, entrepreneur, and disability rights advocate. She is also a service-disabled US Air Force veteran, full-time wheelchair user, single mother, and the former Ms. Wheelchair USA 2016. Sylvia has visited fifty-seven countries, forty-nine of those as a wheelchair user, and 36 of those solo. She has created three sole proprietorships, a limited liability company, and a non-profit corporation—three of which she still manages single-handedly.

Ms. Longmire is the founder of the award-winning Spin the Globe travel blog, on which she shares her adventures traveling around the world in a power wheelchair. She focuses on the wheelchair accessibility of her destinations, encouraging fellow wheelchair users to explore the world. Her accessible travel writing has been featured in *The New York Times*, *New Mobility* magazine, *The Orlando Sentinel*, and Lonely Planet, she has published two travel photography books, and published the first and only book about wheelchair accessible cruising. Through her travel agency (Spin the Globe/Travel), she is making accessible travel dreams come true for fellow wheelchair users and their families.

Ms. Longmire is also a subject matter expert on Mexico's drug war and border security. She is a frequent guest on major media outlets, providing interviews for CNN, MSBNC, FOX News, NBC Nightly News, and more. Ms. Longmire has been a guest expert on The History Channel's *Brad Meltzer's Decoded* and *America's War on Drugs*, and has also consulted for producers of the National Geographic Channel's *Border Wars* and *Drugs, Inc.* series. She is the author of two books on these issues.

Ms. Longmire is the President and founder of The PreJax Foundation, a 501(c)(3) non-profit that provides scholarships to exceptional students who either have multiple sclerosis or a parent with MS. In December 2019, she was selected as a brand ambassador for *O, The Oprah* Magazine for 2020. She is a single mother to two amazing boys and resides in Central Florida.

FOLLOW SYLVIA LONGMIRE

SPIN THE GLOBE
http://www.spintheglobe.net/

FACEBOOK
Facebook.com/spintheglobeonwheels

INSTAGRAM
Instagram.com/sylvia_longmire

TWITTER
Twitter.com/spin_theglobe

YOUTUBE
Youtube.com/smlongmire

OTHER BOOKS BY SYLVIA LONGMIRE

Everything You Need to Know About Wheelchair Accessible Cruising

The View from Down Here II

The View from Down Here

Border Insecurity: Why Big Money, Fences, and Drones Aren't Making Us Safer

Cartel: The Coming Invasion of Mexico's Drug Wars

Made in the USA
Monee, IL
04 November 2026

67375592R00036